"Simplicity is the ultimate sophistication."
Leonardo da Vinci

CONCEPT

"MINIMALISM IS NOT ABOUT HAVING LESS. IT'S ABOUT MAKING ROOM FOR WHAT MATTERS MOST."

The Minimalist Path is a gentle and practical guide designed for people who are overwhelmed by clutter—physically, mentally, and emotionally. It's not a harsh or radical take on minimalism, but a welcoming journey toward clarity, focus, and peace.

THIS BOOK HELPS YOU:

- Simplify your home and mind
- Let go of unnecessary things (and thoughts)
- Create beautiful, purposeful spaces
- Live with more intention and less stress

INTRODUCTION

When Less Becomes Freedom

Why a minimalist lifestyle is the new luxury.

A calm mind begins with a clear space.

CHAPTER 1 – Minimalism Begins in the Mind
- The silent weight of mental clutter
- Slowing down in a fast world
- Learning to prioritize what truly matters

CHAPTER 2 – A Home That Hugs You
- Room-by-room decluttering checklist
- Turning your home into a space of calm
- Light, air, and intentional design

CHAPTER 3 – Fewer Things, Greater Freedom
- Escaping the trap of constant consumption
- How to shop intentionally
- Capsule wardrobes and personal organization

CHAPTER 4 – Minimalism in Routines and Relationships
- Saying "no" without guilt
- Detoxing your schedule and your social life
- Choosing presence over perfection

CHAPTER 5 – Purposeful Decoration
- Decorating with soul, not stuff
- Real-life minimalist room examples

CHAPTER 6 – Living the Minimalist Lifestyle
- How to stay consistent with ease
- 10 daily habits of a modern minimalist
- Building a weekly plan that energizes you

CHAPTER 1 – MINIMALISM BEGINS IN THE MIND

- The silent weight of mental clutter

Not all clutter is physical.
Mental clutter is the constant noise in your mind — unfinished tasks, worries about the future, regrets from the past, information overload, and negative self-talk. It's invisible to others, but it drains your energy every day.

You may not even notice it at first. But soon, you feel tired, unfocused, anxious — and disconnected. You walk into a room and forget why. You scroll endlessly on your phone but feel emptier afterward. That's mental clutter in action.

Minimalism helps clear that noise.
By removing distractions, simplifying your environment, and creating space to breathe, you allow your mind to rest and reset. You start to hear your own thoughts more clearly — not the chaos, but the calm underneath.

To start clearing your mental clutter:
Write down everything that's on your mind — make it visible.
Let go of what's out of your control.
Say "no" more often.
Take five minutes daily to do absolutely nothing — just breathe.

The goal isn't to have a perfect mind.
The goal is to give your mind room to focus, feel, and think freely again.

- Slowing Down in a Fast World

We live in a world that rewards speed. Fast food. Fast internet. Fast results.
We're told that if we're not moving quickly, we're falling behind.
But always rushing creates stress, disconnection, and exhaustion. Life starts to feel like a race we never signed up for.

Slowing down is not laziness — it's wisdom.

It's choosing to be present instead of distracted. To enjoy your coffee instead of gulping it. To take a walk without a podcast. To talk without checking your phone.

When you slow down, your senses wake up.
You hear your thoughts again. You notice beauty in small things.
You give your mind and body permission to breathe.

Minimalism isn't just about owning less. It's about living slower, deeper, and more intentionally — even in a fast world.

- Learning to Prioritize What Truly Matters

When your home is full of things you don't use, need, or love — it becomes a place of stress, not rest.
We often keep items out of guilt, habit, or "just in case." But these things quietly steal our time, energy, and space.
A cluttered home reflects a cluttered mind.
Minimalism isn't about having an empty house — it's about keeping only what supports the life you want.

Ask yourself:
    Do I use this?
    Do I love this?
    Does this make my life easier or more beautiful?
If not, let it go — with   gratitude.
Prioritizing what matters means choosing items that serve a purpose or spark peace. Fewer items. More meaning.

Start small:
One drawer. One shelf. One room.
Keep what aligns with who you are today — not who you were, or who you "might be someday."

CHAPTER 2 – A HOME THAT HUGS YOU

- Room-by-Room Decluttering Checklist

LIVING ROOM

- ☐ Remove items you don't use daily (old remotes, unused décor)
- ☐ Keep only meaningful or calming decorations
- ☐ Limit books/magazines to a small, intentional selection
- ☐ Clear coffee tables and shelves — leave space to breathe
- ☐ Store blankets and pillows neatly

KITCHEN

- [ ] Toss expired food and unused spices
- [ ] Keep only the utensils and gadgets you actually use
- [ ] Declutter the junk drawer
- [ ] Minimize mugs, plates, and storage containers
- [ ] Wipe counters and store appliances off the surface

BEDROOM

- [ ] Remove clothes you haven't worn in 6–12 months
- [ ] Keep only 1 or 2 sets of bedding
- [ ] Clear bedside tables — keep only essentials
- [ ] Store personal items out of sight for a peaceful feel
- [ ] Donate shoes or accessories that no longer serve you

Tip: Don't aim for perfection

—

aim for peace. Decluttering is a gift to your future self.

BATHROOM

- [ ] Throw out old or empty toiletries
- [ ] Keep just one of each item you use (shampoo, lotion, etc.)
- [ ] Store items in labeled baskets or drawers
- [ ] Keep surfaces clean and minimal
- [ ] Get rid of old towels or those you don't like to use

WORKSPACE OR OFFICE

- [ ] Recycle old papers and mail
- [ ] Keep desk surfaces clear — one pen, one notebook, one goal
- [ ] Organize cables and tech accessories
- [ ] Minimize decorative items — focus = peace
- [ ] Keep only what supports your current work

KIDS' AREA

- [ ] Donate toys no longer played with
- [ ] Keep toys in bins or baskets for easy access
- [ ] Rotate toys weekly to reduce visual clutter
- [ ] Store sentimental items in a memory box
- [ ] Involve kids: ask what they love most!

- Turning your home into a space of calm

Your home is not just where you sleep.
It's where you think.
It's where you recover.
It's where you breathe after a long, difficult day.
When the outside world feels chaotic, your home should not reflect the same stress.
It should protect your peace — not add to the pressure.

Mental Clarity Starts at Home, example:
Imagine coming home from work and seeing piles of laundry, cluttered countertops, and loud colors everywhere.

Instead of relaxing, your brain starts processing:
   "I need to clean that."
   "Why is this mess still here?"
   "I don't even know where to start..."
This creates mental fatigue.
But now imagine walking into a room with soft light, clear surfaces, and only a few peaceful items.

Your brain immediately feels:
   "I can rest here."
   "Everything has its place."
   "This is peace."

Your Environment Affects Your Sleep, example:
A messy bedroom with too much stuff, screens, or noise makes it harder for your mind to shut down.
But a clean, minimal bedroom with soft light, no clutter, and fresh air?
You fall asleep faster. You stay asleep longer. You wake up less stressed.

Relationships Improve in a Calm Home, when your space is chaotic, it's easier to get irritated or argue. But a calm home invites calm communication.
Less stress = more kindness.

> *"A clear dining table creates space for real conversation — not just meals in silence or in front of a screen."*

Creativity Grows in Quiet Spaces, if your home is full of distractions, your ideas get lost. But in a peaceful space, your mind has room to wander — to dream, to write, to build.
Many great writers, artists, and thinkers work in clean, minimal spaces. That's no accident.

A calm home isn't about perfection. It's about support.
It should support your peace, your dreams, your relationships, your mental health, and minimalism is the tool that helps make that happen — room by room, object by object. Your outer world reflects your inner world. When you clean your space, you clean your mind.

- Light, air, and intentional design

The Foundations of a Calm and Inspiring Home
A peaceful home is not only about what you remove — it's about what you welcome in and the three most powerful elements you can invite are:

1. Natural Light
2. Fresh Air
3. Intentional Design

1. Natural Light – Let Your Space Breathe
Light affects your energy, your focus, your mood.
Dark, closed spaces can feel heavy and depressing. But light-filled rooms feel alive.

"A bright room helps create a bright mind."

Tips:
- Open curtains fully during the day.
- Use sheer or light-colored fabrics.
- Place mirrors across from windows to reflect light.
- Avoid blocking windows with furniture or clutter.
-

2. Fresh Air – Clear Air, Clear Thoughts
A well-ventilated home is essential for calm and clarity. Stale air makes you tired, irritable, even anxious and fresh air resets your mood.
It brings the outside in. It helps you think.

Tips:
- Open windows daily, even for just 15 minutes.
- Add plants — they clean the air and calm the mind.
- Use natural scents like eucalyptus or lavender instead of heavy perfumes.

3. Intentional Design – Every Object Has Purpose, a calm home is not full of random items, it's filled with things that serve a function or bring peace.

Intentional design means:
- Choosing fewer, better pieces of furniture.
- Decorating with meaning, not just filling space.
- Creating flow — easy movement and breathing room in each area.

Example: *A minimalist desk with just a notebook, lamp, and plant invites focus.*
A cluttered desk with wires, papers, and distractions blocks your mind.

"Your home is your energy source. When it feels light, you feel light."

CHAPTER 3 – FEWER THINGS, GREATER FREEDOM

- Escaping the trap of constant consumption

We live in a world that tells us we are one purchase away from happiness.
Every scroll, every ad, every suggestion says:
"Buy this, and you'll feel better."
"Add this to your home, and you'll feel complete."
But here's the truth: The more we consume without intention, the more we feel overwhelmed, not only in our homes — but in our minds, our routines, and our peace.
The Hidden Cost of Overconsumption
Every item we bring home requires something from us:
- Time to clean it
- Space to store it
- Energy to maintain it
- Money to buy it

What starts as a "good deal" ends up costing you freedom. Soon your kitchen drawers are full. Your closets are bursting. Your schedule is packed with the stress of managing things you no longer even use.
This is not abundance, it's exhaustion in disguise.
Cluttered Home = Cluttered Mind
Have you ever walked into a messy room and instantly felt anxious or tired?
That's not a coincidence. Visual clutter leads to mental noise.
When there are too many things in your space, your brain works harder to process your surroundings.

You feel more distracted, less focused, and often emotionally drained.
Clearing your space is not just about aesthetics — it's about mental health.
Breaking the Cycle, the trap of consumption is not just about buying things.
It's about filling voids.

- We shop when we feel bored.
- We scroll when we feel disconnected.
- We order more when we feel stressed.

But these are temporary fixes for deeper needs: connection, peace, purpose.
The minimalist path invites you to pause and ask:
"What am I really looking for?"
Because no item on a shelf will replace inner calm.

A Life with Fewer Things and Greater Meaning
Imagine waking up in a room that feels open and clean. You know where everything is, every object has purpose and peace you don't spend your time sorting piles. You spend your time living.
This is what happens when you stop consuming and start curating.

- Fewer but better clothes
- Fewer but meaningful decorations
- Fewer distractions, more presence

Tips to Escape the Consumption Trap:

- Create a 48-hour rule before buying anything

→ Wait. If you still need it after 2 days, buy it. If not, it was just impulse.

2. Unsubscribe from marketing emails and alerts
→ Reduce temptation from your inbox.

3. Declutter before you shop
→ When you see what you already have, you stop wanting more.

4. Practice gratitude for what you own
→ Gratitude reduces the urge to constantly chase newness.

Conclusion: **Choose Intention Over Impulse**

Escaping the trap of constant consumption doesn't mean living with nothing.

It means living with what matters.

Minimalism teaches us that joy doesn't come from what we buy — it comes from how we live.

So the next time you're tempted to click "buy now", ask yourself:

"Do I need this — or am I trying to feel something?"

Because peace doesn't come in a package. It comes from letting go.

- How to shop intentionally

In a culture of fast clicks and one-day shipping, shopping has become automatic.

But minimalism teaches us that buying with intention is a skill — and a mindset.

Intentional shopping is not about depriving yourself.

It's about choosing quality over quantity, value over impulse, and purpose over clutter.

Step 1: Understand the "Why" Before the "Buy"

Before you add something to your cart, ask yourself:
- Why do I want this?
- Do I truly need it — or am I just reacting to emotion (boredom, stress, comparison)?
- Is this a short-term desire or a long-term need?

Awareness kills impulse.

The moment you pause to reflect, you're already shopping more intentionally.

Step 2: Make a List — And Stick to It

Just like grocery shopping, life shopping needs a plan.
- Keep a running list of things you actually need.
- If something new comes to mind, wait 48 hours before buying.
- Ask: "Would I still want this if I didn't see it on sale?"

A list creates boundaries — and boundaries create freedom.

Step 3: Focus on Quality and Longevity
Minimalists don't just buy less.
They buy better.
Ask:
- Is this well-made?
- Will this last more than one season?
- Am I willing to repair this instead of replace it?

One quality item can replace five cheap ones — and reduce waste, cost, and stress in the long run.

Step 4: Think About the Space It Will Occupy
Before buying, imagine exactly where it will live in your home.
If it has no clear purpose or place, it will become clutter.
Ask:
- Will I use this often?
- Do I have to create space for this item?
- Is it adding peace or taking energy?

Step 5: Set a Monthly "Mindful Spending" Budget
Even minimalists spend money — they just spend it intentionally.
- Give yourself a "mindful spending" amount each month.
- Use it for things that bring real joy or solve real problems.
- Track what you spend and reflect at the end of each month.

Intentional shopping becomes a habit when you track your values with your money.

Step 6: Unfollow, Unsubscribe, Unplug
Many buying urges aren't yours — they're planted.
- Unsubscribe from promo emails and shopping apps
- Turn off "one-click" shortcuts
- Avoid aimless scrolling that leads to "add to cart" moments

The fewer ads you see, the fewer impulses you fight.

Step 7: Choose Alignment Over Attraction
When something tempts you, ask:
"Does this align with the life I'm building?"
If it doesn't support your values, your peace, or your vision — let it go.
Intentional shopping isn't about saying "no" to everything.
It's about saying "yes" to the right things.

- Capsule Wardrobes and Personal Organization

A cluttered wardrobe often leads to a cluttered mind. Each morning, we face a wall of clothes, many of which we no longer wear, like, or even remember buying. Decision fatigue begins in the closet — and it follows us through the day.
That's where the capsule wardrobe comes in.
A capsule wardrobe is a small, intentional collection of clothing that reflects your style, fits your life, and works together in harmony. Instead of quantity, it offers clarity. Instead of chaos, it brings control.
Imagine opening your closet and knowing that every piece fits you well, feels comfortable, and matches everything else. It saves time, reduces stress, and makes daily decisions easier — all while freeing space in your mind and home.
But capsule wardrobes are not just about clothes — they represent a new way of living. They teach us to:

- Let go of what no longer serves us.
- Focus on quality over trends.
- Choose function and simplicity over excess.

To create a capsule wardrobe, you don't need to throw everything away. You start by observing what you actually wear, what you feel good in, and what aligns with your day-to-day reality. Keep the essentials — the versatile pieces that you love and use often. Let go of the rest, guilt-free.
This process isn't just about fashion. It's a powerful exercise in self-awareness and personal organization. As you curate your closet, you begin to curate your time, your energy, your priorities.

CHAPTER 4 – MINIMALISM IN ROUTINES AND RELATIONSHIPS

- Saying "No" Without Guilt

In today's fast-paced and demanding world, where expectations often outweigh personal well-being, learning to say "no" without guilt is one of the most powerful and freeing habits you can develop. Minimalism is not just about decluttering physical items—it's about removing the mental and emotional excess that keeps you from living intentionally. One of the biggest sources of this excess is the pressure to always be available, agreeable, and constantly "on." Whether it's saying yes to social invitations you don't enjoy, accepting work you don't have time for, or agreeing to favors out of obligation, each unnecessary "yes" is a quiet denial of your own peace and priorities.

When you choose minimalism, you choose to protect your time and energy. Saying "no" becomes a natural extension of that choice. It's not about rejection—it's about alignment. When you say no to something that doesn't serve your purpose, you're saying yes to rest, to space, to clarity. You're making room for what truly matters, whether that's meaningful relationships, deep focus, personal health, or simply silence. Saying "no" without guilt is an act of respect—not only for yourself, but for the life you are choosing to create.

This discipline helps you recognize that your attention is a limited resource, and that you're not obligated to explain or justify every boundary. A simple, honest "no, thank you" is often enough. As you grow in this mindset, you begin to feel the difference between being busy and being fulfilled, between being surrounded and truly connected. In time, guilt fades, and what replaces it is something far more powerful: confidence, peace, and an unwavering commitment to the life you truly want.

- Detoxing your schedule and your social life

We often think of detoxing as something we do for our bodies—removing toxins, cleansing the system, starting fresh. But what if your schedule and your social life are also overloaded with "toxins"? Overcommitments, empty obligations, draining relationships, and constant busyness can weigh just as heavily on your mental and emotional well-being as physical clutter. A minimalist lifestyle invites you to look at your time the same way you look at your space: with intention, clarity, and care.

Detoxing your schedule means giving yourself permission to let go of what no longer adds value to your days. That recurring meeting you always dread? That weekly commitment that brings more stress than joy? That habit of saying yes before you've even thought it through? All of these moments add up to a life that feels rushed, fragmented, and disconnected. When you begin to clear your calendar the same way you would clean out a cluttered room, something powerful happens—you begin to breathe again. You create space for what truly matters, whether it's quiet mornings, quality time with loved ones, or the ability to focus deeply without interruption.

The same principle applies to your social life. Minimalism doesn't mean isolating yourself; it means being deeply intentional with the energy you invest in relationships. Instead of spreading yourself thin across dozens of shallow connections, you begin to nurture the few that are meaningful, mutual, and uplifting. You learn to recognize which friendships energize you and which drain you—and you act accordingly, without guilt.

This kind of detox isn't about cutting people or plans for the sake of it. It's about realignment. It's choosing presence over performance, depth over quantity, peace over constant motion. When your days are no longer filled with noise and pressure, you begin to hear something else—your own thoughts, your real needs, your authentic desires.

A minimalist approach to time and relationships invites you to live with clarity and intention, making sure that every hour and every connection reflects who you truly are and where you're truly going. Less obligation, more purpose. Less noise, more meaning.

- Choosing presence over perfection

it's easy to fall into the trap of chasing perfection. We're taught to believe that everything must be flawless—our homes, our careers, our bodies, even our routines. But perfection is not only unattainable; it's also exhausting. It steals joy from the present moment and replaces it with pressure, anxiety, and self-doubt. Minimalism challenges this mindset by offering something much more liberating: presence.

Choosing presence over perfection means embracing where you are, as you are, without needing everything to be finished, polished, or impressive. It means noticing the way sunlight hits your kitchen table in the morning, even if that table isn't perfectly clean. It's about sitting with your child or partner in the middle of a messy house and realizing that this—this connection, this laughter, this pause—is what actually matters.

When you let go of the need to perfect every detail, you create space to fully live. You stop rearranging constantly and start appreciating intentionally. You cook without needing the meal to be Instagram-worthy. You welcome guests into your home without apologizing for the unfolded laundry. You take action on your goals even when conditions aren't ideal—because showing up matters more than waiting for everything to be right.

Presence invites authenticity. It reminds you that real life is textured and imperfect, and that beauty lives in the raw and unfiltered.

The minimalist path encourages you to strip away not just physical clutter, but also mental expectations that weigh you down. The more you practice being present—with yourself, with others, with your surroundings—the more peace you'll find. You'll begin to measure success not by what you achieve or perfect, but by how fully you experience each moment.

In the end, presence is where life actually happens. It's where joy is felt, where clarity emerges, and where true change begins. Choosing presence over perfection isn't about settling for less— it's about finally seeing that less is exactly what allows you to feel more.

CHAPTER 5 – PURPOSEFUL DECORATION

- Decorating with Soul, Not Stuff

Minimalist decor doesn't mean cold or empty — it means intentional, meaningful spaces. Your home should reflect who you are, not just what you own. Here's how to bring soul into your space without clutter:

1. Choose meaning over quantity
Instead of filling shelves with trendy decor, select items that tell a story.
- A painting you created
- A photo from a meaningful trip
- A gift from someone you love
- Fewer items, but more personal value.

2. Incorporate natural elements
Nature brings warmth and peace.
- Add plants, wood textures, linen, or natural light.
- These elements make your space feel alive and calming.

3. Use fewer pieces with greater impact
- A large statement vase
- A unique mirror
- A handcrafted candle
- Each piece should have presence and intentional placement.

4. Let color reflect your mood
- Neutral tones promote peace and clarity
- Add small touches of color to show your personality
- Keep the palette harmonious to support emotional balance

5. Let functional items be beautiful
- A wooden ladder as a shelf
- A woven basket for blankets
- Stylish kitchenware on open shelves
- Function can enhance form when chosen with care.

6. Leave room for emptiness
Empty space is not a flaw — it's breathing room.
- It allows your home to feel open and your mind to feel calm
- Blank walls and clear surfaces invite peace

Decorating with soul creates a home that is inspiring, calming, and true to you. It's not about more things — it's about the right things.

- Real-Life Minimalist Room Examples

Minimalism it's about clarity, purpose, and beauty through simplicity. Here are a few real-life examples that show how different rooms can embody the minimalist philosophy while remaining warm, functional, and full of soul.

1. The Living Room – Calm Meets Comfort
A small sofa in a neutral tone, a single piece of art above it, a woven rug, and a houseplant in the corner. Natural light filters in through sheer curtains. There's no clutter — just open space, a place to breathe, read, and relax. Books are stacked neatly in a small shelf, and the coffee table holds only a candle and a favorite magazine.

2. The Bedroom – A Space to Truly Rest
A low wooden bed frame, soft white bedding, and just two pillows. On each side, simple nightstands with soft lamps. No TV, no extra furniture. A framed photo on the wall adds a personal touch. The feeling is intentional: this is a room for sleeping, reflecting, and recharging.

3. The Kitchen – Function First, Always
Open shelves display a few beautiful, often-used dishes. The counters are mostly clear, except for a coffee maker and a fruit bowl. Drawers are organized, and only what's used daily is kept out. A calm color palette — soft grey, wood, and white — keeps the room feeling open and clean.

4. The Home Office – Clarity to Create
A small desk with only a laptop, notebook, and pen. A chair that supports posture. A vision board or plant adds focus and grounding. The space is quiet, free from distraction — a corner where ideas grow.

5. The Bathroom – Serenity in Simplicity
A walk-in shower with glass walls. A wooden tray holds a bar of soap, a scrub, and a candle. Towels are folded on an open shelf. The room is bright, natural, and spa-like — proof that even the smallest spaces can offer peace.

These rooms prove that minimalism isn't cold — it's warm, focused, and intentional. It's not about what's missing — it's about what truly matters being present. Each space supports your well-being, not your stress. And that's the heart of minimalist living.

CHAPTER 6 – LIVING THE MINIMALIST LIFESTYLE

- How to Stay Consistent with Ease

Consistency doesn't have to be hard. In fact, when you live minimally, staying consistent becomes a natural rhythm — not a forced effort. The reason many people struggle to maintain habits is because their lives are cluttered with too many options, distractions, and unnecessary commitments. Minimalism removes the noise.

When your space is clean, your schedule is light, and your goals are clear, it becomes easier to show up for yourself every day. You no longer waste energy deciding what to wear, where to begin, or what matters most — because your surroundings and routines are already aligned with your priorities.
The key is to design your life in a way that supports your values. Choose habits that feel sustainable, not extreme. Start your morning the same way each day. Keep your to-do list short but focused. Use visual cues — like a tidy workspace or a single daily journal — to stay on track.

Consistency becomes ease when your environment reminds you who you want to be. When everything you own and everything you do has a purpose, you're no longer battling chaos — you're moving forward with clarity.
Minimalism is not about perfection. It's about making it easy to do the right thing, often. And from that ease comes powerful transformation.

- 10 Daily Habits of a Modern Minimalist

1. Start the day with clarity
Instead of reaching for your phone, a minimalist starts with stillness — a few moments to breathe, stretch, or journal. This sets the tone for intentional living, not reactive living.

2. Dress simply, with purpose
No more wardrobe stress. Minimalists curate a capsule closet, where every piece fits well and feels good. Getting dressed is fast, effortless, and confident.

3. Clear the physical clutter
Every day, even if for five minutes, they tidy their space. A clear desk, an empty sink, or a reset living room supports mental calm.

4. Stick to a simple to-do list
Minimalists don't overload their day. They choose 2-3 meaningful tasks and focus on them deeply. Less rush, more results.

5. Practice conscious consumption
They pause before buying. "Do I need this? Does it align with my values?" This daily awareness protects their space, time, and wallet.

6. Check in with their mental space
A minimalist doesn't just declutter their home — they declutter their thoughts. Through journaling, meditation, or silence, they protect their inner peace.

7. Set boundaries with technology
They limit mindless scrolling and turn off non-essential notifications. They use tech with purpose, not distraction.

8. Enjoy slow moments intentionally
Minimalists find joy in small things — making tea, walking, reading a real book. Slowing down isn't lazy. It's nourishing.

9. Express gratitude, daily
They take time to notice what's good. Gratitude grounds them in the present and keeps desires in check.
10. Reflect and reset
At the end of each day, they reflect. "What brought me peace today? What drained me?" This habit helps them live better, not just more.

These habits are not rules — they're reminders. Small daily choices shape a minimalist lifestyle that brings more freedom, focus, and fulfillment.

- Building a weekly plan that energizes you

A minimalist lifestyle isn't about doing less — it's about doing what matters most. That's why your weekly plan should energize you, not exhaust you.
Instead of overfilling your calendar with endless obligations, a minimalist creates a flexible structure that prioritizes clarity, rest, and momentum. You begin by identifying your non-negotiables: sleep, nourishing meals, exercise, meaningful work, and connection with people you love. These are your foundation.
Next, you intentionally schedule deep work and deep rest. You don't just react to the week — you design it. Leave space between tasks. Avoid back-to-back meetings. Build in quiet mornings or early evenings for reflection. Block time for creativity, movement, and even nothing at all.
A good weekly plan is like a well-designed room — everything has a purpose, and there's enough breathing space to feel alive in it.
When your week reflects your values, you don't burn out. You grow, gently but consistently.

Final Thoughts
What Awaits You After This Journey

As you reach the final page of The Minimalist Path, know that this isn't the end — it's the beginning of something quieter, clearer, and more fulfilling.

Minimalism isn't just about having less. It's about gaining more of what truly matters: more time, more peace, more focus, more intention. As you begin to apply these ideas — decluttering your home, simplifying your routines, making conscious choices — you'll notice subtle but powerful shifts.

Your mind will feel calmer.
Your space will feel lighter.
Your days will have more breathing room.

You'll find yourself saying "no" without guilt, choosing rest without shame, and experiencing moments with a new sense of clarity. This lifestyle gently but steadily reduces stress and anxiety. It gives you back the most precious thing: time — time to think, to create, to connect, and to live more fully.

Let this book be your reset button.

And from here on, walk lighter, live slower, and create space — not just in your home, but in your life.
You don't need to be perfect to begin.
You just need to begin.

"The beauty of life is found in the simplicity of each choice."